PRIVATE LOGIC

UNCOVERING
A TRUNKFUL OF GOLD

Lynn Lott

Barbara Mendenhall

Emily Wang

EC

Official manual for the certified training
ENCOURAGEMENT CONSULTANT by Lynn Lott

ISBN 978-1-7340820-0-5 (paperback)

ISBN 978-1-7340820-1-2 (ebook)

First printing, 2020.

Lynn Lott Encouragement Consulting

www.lynnlottec.com

Table of Contents

Introduction

Uncover the Past, Understand the Present, and Create a Different Future

A beggar had been begging for 30 years and believed that it would be his whole life. One day, a stranger passed by and saw the beggar holding up the hat and mumbling, "Have mercy and pity please, give me some money."

The stranger said, "I have nothing for you." And then he asked, "What are you sitting on?"

The beggar replied, "It is nothing, only an old trunk. I have been sitting on it forever."

The stranger asked, "Have you ever opened the trunk?"

"No, never," the beggar said. "What is the point? There is nothing in it."

The stranger insisted, "Open the trunk and have a look."

The beggar, having nothing better to do, opened the trunk. To his great surprise and joy, there was a trunk full of gold. The beggar had believed his whole life that he was poor and asking for help without realizing that he had been sitting on a trunkful of gold!

It is a perfect metaphor for life. Many of us search for answers, expecting others to help us and guide us, without realizing that we are already sitting on a trunk full of childhood memories, which are our greatest treasure. There is gold in our memories.

Childhood memories contain our road map for future life. The dilemmas we encounter in adult life start with our childhood experience. The memories are there to alert us to possible harm or to encourage us to continue with a certain pattern of thinking and doing. We can't change what we have decided in childhood without being aware of those decisions and then taking initiative.

Emily felt troubled about going to Shanghai (in her mind, the Manhattan of China) to give a training. She said, "I thought Shanghai people were chic and mean, and I would be laughed at or treated unkindly. Even though I had been living in Beijing for 13 years, a modern and fashionable college teacher and a successful trainer and business owner, I was uncomfortable about going."

To get some help with my dilemma, I thought back to my childhood memories.

I remembered when I was a village girl and moved to the city to live with my grandparents to go to a better middle school. One day, my head teacher went to visit my grandma and said, "You should take Emily to have a haircut and then ask her to wash her hair more often." I remember feeling surprised and ashamed. I did not really fit in with the city teenagers. In my memory, the city was beautiful and clean, while I was not clean and not chic. I felt afraid and insecure.

Once I saw my 'Shanghai complex' in my memory, I pictured using a magic wand, and I changed my memory. I saw myself being happy, surrounded by a group of not-so-clean teenagers, fooling around and laughing." Childhood memories can be changed if you happen to have a magic wand nearby (a magic pencil can work in place of a magic wand)!

That is the best part of working with these memories. We can change the road map we drew as children, which opens us to new possibilities as adults. We can create new endings to our stories.

Do you have a memory now?

What is the memory telling you?

What can you learn from your memory about your present trouble?

Imagine this. You're three years old. Your parents have just come home from the hospital with a new sibling. They are holding the baby and smiling and talking baby talk and kissing the baby. They say to you, "Look, you have a new brother. Come and give your brother a kiss." You run crying to another room, lie on the floor, kick your feet, pound your fists and refuse to get up.

What are you thinking in that moment? Here's a guess: "If I was good enough, why did they have to have another baby? They don't love me or want me." It's entirely possible that you or any other three-year-old might think this way, and no matter what anyone tells you, you'd be pretty sure you were right.

This is the beginning of private logic. It's your unconscious response to what is happening around you — what you decided as a child and believe even now that you are an adult. At a very young age, sometimes even before they have language, children make decisions they don't know they are making. Once made, the decisions get tucked away in the brain until "needed" to help make sense out of the world. We call these decisions *private logic* or *operating system*, and they are unique to each person.[1]

---

1   We use private logic and operating system interchangeably.

Forming your private logic as an infant or toddler helps you explain and understand the world around you. It doesn't mean you're right, but it's entirely possible that you believe your thoughts and unknowingly carry them with you as you go through life.

Despite what conventional wisdom says about the influence of genetics (nature) and environment (nurture) on developing personality – and to be sure, these play a part — *it is your creative interpretation, your unconscious decisions about what is happening around you that best explains how you formed your private logic.* No one made you think the way you think and you didn't inherit your thoughts. Life happened; you needed to make sense out of it; at a very early age, you had no idea you were creating a complex system of explaining who you were, others were, life was, and how you needed to behave. Your private logic is that pattern of reaction and interaction between you and life.

We call it *private logic* because it is personal and individual. It contains your beliefs about what you, others and life are or should be like, as well as what you therefore must or should be doing. Your system works to a point, but particularly as you become an adult it may not work as well. If unchallenged, your private logic limits your life choices and possibilities. If you are stuck and controlled by an operating system to live your life one way only, you may have conflicts with all kinds of relationships. If you want to have more choices and more possibilities, you need to upgrade your operating system!

Fortunately, you can make new decisions which can lead to new behaviors and new outcomes. The method we use is to help you make friends with your inner child, learn what that child decided, thinks and feels, and finally, how to encourage the child to grow up.

In the following chapters, you'll learn how to discover your own private logic and to use what we call the three A's – Awareness, Acceptance and Action to improve your life and relationships. You'll see how others have applied the same process to address current issues and solve problems.

One

Discovering Your Inner Child

The crux of this book is to help you uncover your private logic – what you decided as a child that you didn't know you were deciding, to be **aware** of it, and to **accept** that this is what you decided and that your behavior has been based on how you once decided to solve life's problems. With this awareness of your past and acceptance of how it shapes your present reality and situation, you will finally see the whole picture unfolded in front of you, and you will have opportunities to take **action** to help you create a better future outcome, with an upgraded operating system. Awareness, Acceptance and Action are what we call the Three A's - your steps to change.

The process that we recommend for discovering and advancing your private logic is easy. First *think of a current issue or problem you are struggling with*. Then let yourself have a childhood memory, even if the memory doesn't seem to be connected or make sense. Write down the memory. You have now discovered your inner child! When you are writing your memory, be sure to start with the phrase, "I remember one time…" instead of, "We always used to…" For example, you can learn a lot more about your private logic from the statement, "I remember one time I went to Grandma's house and she made fried baloney for me. I felt loved and I decided that I'm pretty special," rather than sharing memories which sound like, "My grandma used to make me fried baloney."

To *make friends with your inner child*, pretend the memory belongs to someone else, and make a list of guesses about how that person might view themselves, others, life and, therefore, how they solve problems. Write down your guesses. If you have a group of friends or family to brainstorm guesses with you, even better. Just make sure you, or someone helping you, writes them all down. This step helps you learn how your inner child thinks and feels. To *encourage your inner child* and *help the inner child to grow up*, look at the list of guesses and circle those that, in that moment, seem most "right" to you.

Next, ask yourself, *if nothing changes, how will problems and issues like the current one look in your future?* Write down the answer.

Now that you're aware of what you decided, can you accept that without judgement in order to help the child within you to grow up?

Accepting is often the hardest of the three A's. You can always say to yourself, "It is what it is; I love you no matter what; or what happened is what happened, and it does not have to be the pattern for my whole life. It's an essential step you need to take before you're ready to create an action plan to form your new path to the future.

To create an action plan, you can get advice, assistance or another perspective to create your plan. Here are some suggestions for how to do that.

- You can imagine that, as an adult, you hold the little child inside you on your lap or sit next to her on the couch, offering encouragement.

- You can use the Madame Dora cards, pulling one at random. Read the advice on the card and apply what you can to your private logic or current situation.

- You can use a real or pretend magic wand. Ask yourself, "If I had a magic wand, how would I change things?" Make a list of possible changes you could make. Choose one or two and try them out for a day or a week. Write down your "changes" so you can go back and look at them at the end of a week and assess your progress and learning. Write that down, too.

- You can also simply ask for ideas from someone you trust who understands that you want to help your inner child grow up.

Here is an example of how one person used this process to learn about the thoughts, feelings, and behaviors she was currently experiencing because her "inner child" was in charge of her life and calling the shots.

Francie: Sibling Rivalry

Present
Current Issue: Francie hated the adult relationship she had with her brother, five years younger. She didn't like how she felt and acted toward him. As a family visit approached, she was wondering how she could communicate better and improve her relationship with him.

Past
Childhood Memory: As she looked for the private logic that might be

keeping her stuck, the childhood memory that came to Francie was this: "I was a teenager. My parents had gone to work and my brother and I stayed at home. I was taking care of him and washing clothes at the same time. I thought he didn't have to do any chores like I did and I felt angry. So I came up with an idea to get even. I hid behind a wall and he couldn't find me and he was scared and cried. Right at that moment I reappeared. But I also felt guilty because he was crying."

Francie's Private Logic *(Guesses about Francie's beliefs about "I," "Others," "Life" and "Therefore")*:

We suggested some beliefs the child inside her might still be harboring, keeping her stuck with her brother:

- I feel angry when I have to be responsible for others and do more than they do.

- Others are smaller than me.

- Others need and depend on me.

- Life is unfair.

- Therefore I find ways to get even and then I feel guilty.

We asked Francie if she could see how the thinking of the child inside her could be messing with her shot at better relationships today. She was clear about the connection, saying, "I have the same feeling as in the memory in the current situation. I see what he isn't doing, how he's still goofing off and not really growing up or becoming independent, not taking care of himself, much less of anyone else. I feel angry but also guilty about judging him."

Future

If nothing changes, how will this be for her in the future? Francie said, "I will behave nicely but our communication will be on a very superficial level. When I try to have a conversation about his current life, the atmosphere will probably be tense and we'll both feel weird."

3 A's

Next, we asked Francie to talk about "the *3 A's*". Here is what she said:

Awareness: "I still relate to my brother like his second mother and feel guilty that I might have influenced how he is now. Even though my training is helping me learn to be more accepting, deep inside I still feel angry."

Acceptance: "I was and still am typical of many first-born kids in the way they think of and treat a younger sibling. Haha! I'm totally normal! We each have had influence and impact on the other, but it's no one's fault."

Action: "I've been working too hard lately. I want to just relax and stop sacrificing myself for others. I want to simply enjoy our visit and not think too much."

Advice

We asked if Francie wanted to see what Madame Dora would say about her situation, and she agreed. The card she pulled was Confrontational Clyde, who said, "No one can be the boss of you when you're the boss of yourself." Francie cracked up, grinning and chuckling – which we call a recognition response. ! She laughed, "Wow. OK. Who knew this was really about my relationship with myself all along?! If I want to encourage my inner Francie who is still about 10 years old, what do I do?"

We suggested to Francie that she remember that, "guilt equals should," and asked her, "What are your 'shoulds'?" She answered, "I should be a better sister, show more concern or care about my brother and I should be more helpful to him." When we operate from "should," we usually feel resentful because it's not what we really want to do. We need to change our "shoulds" to "I want to...", "I'm going to...", "I will...", or "I can...", so we can avoid resentment and move forward with encouragement instead.

Talk to Your Inner Child

In addition, we suggested to Francie that she pretend she was sitting beside the 10-year-old girl inside her and imagine putting her arm around her shoulder. "Tell her, 'It's not easy for you to do so much at such a young age, and it's all right that you're angry. You're just you and you don't need to be responsible for anyone else's life. You are responsible and kind enough.'"

You can download a larger, printable version of the ***Now it's Your Turn*** form here:

https://lynnlottec.com/wp-content/uploads/2020/08/YourTurnForm8.5x11.pdf.

Now It's Your Turn

To learn more about yourself, fill out the template below. Follow the instructions above to guide you. You may want to invite friends or family members to help you, especially with brainstorming when you get the sections called "Private Logic" and "Advice".

Name:_____ Date:_____

Present

Current Issue: _____

_____

Past

Childhood memory: _____

_____

_____

Private Logic:

I _____

Others _____

Life_____

Therefore _____

Future

If Nothing Changes: _____

3 A's

Awareness: _____

Acceptance: _____

Action: _____

Advice

Magic Wand: _____

Madame Dora Card:_____

Thoughts:_____

Talk to Your Inner Child:_____

_____

_____

_____

_____

Two
Tamara: Maintaining a Good Girl Identity

Present

Current Issue: Tamara is working on scheduling with her partner Eliza who is traveling from the West Coast to the East Coast and gone a lot of the time. Eliza is in Boston for ten days a month, and sees her family when she's traveling. Tamara feels jealous and envious of the time Eliza spends traveling and with her family, but she is afraid to tell Eliza any of this.

Past

Childhood Memory: The vivid memory from her childhood that came to Tamara is a good example of how what seems like a random memory is actually related to the current issue. Tamara shared, "I remember this one time when I was probably between 6 and 9 years old, living in Berkeley. We were at Mr. Mops Toy Store. I had just had a birthday party where we gave away little plastic beaded necklaces. I was wearing the necklace I had from the party and got so scared someone was going to think I stole it. I was so scared that I took the necklace off and put it back on the rack in the store."

Tamara's Private Logic: Tamara said, "When I think of why I was so convinced people would think I stole it, I realize that I believed people think the worst of others and it's my job to prove that I'm good. There's that need to be good and to not have people think badly of me. I want everyone to think really highly of me – that I'm good, perfect and wonderful all the time. Sometimes I want to be bad and take things, but I'm afraid someone would see that in me and that's why they would think I stole the necklace. So I believe I must always be good because I care what people think of me and not because I really am good."

Tamara had pretty much nailed down her private logic, so our guesswork was made easy:

- I need to be good.

- I want everyone to think really highly of me.

- I sometimes want to be bad and take things.

- Others see that in me.

- Others think the worst of me.

- Life is a place where it's my job to prove that I'm good.

- Therefore I must always be good, perfect and wonderful so no one thinks badly of me and everyone thinks highly of me.

Future

If Nothing Changes: Tamara realized that if she didn't change the childhood thinking that she still carried inside her, in the future she would run around trying to act good all the time, always making sacrifices to ensure that people think well of her instead of thinking she's a bad person doing bad things. It's a future where she's working extra hard seeking respect and acknowledgement, because she believes that who she is isn't good enough.

Exhausting, right? Here's what Tamara said about the "3 A's":

3 A's

Awareness: "I'm very aware of the fact that so much I have to do is about what people might think. I'm aware that I don't think very highly of myself, my motives or my intentions and I'm aware that I'm running around like crazy trying to manage everyone else and their feelings and thoughts about me. I'm engaged in image management – doing everything I can to manage what people think about me."

Acceptance: "I accept that my motives are centered on managing people's perceptions of me, that I do care about what others think about me, and that I do not act on my occasional wish to be 'selfish' out of concern for my image." At that point, Tamara grimaced, took a deep breath, remarked, "Yikes. All of that is hard to swallow without judgment. But I know acceptance means just recognizing the truth of what is, and not judging it. It just almost stops me in my tracks."

We reminded Tamara that taking action to move forward needs to start from where you are, not from where you wish you were or think you should be.

Action: She said, "I need to work on respecting myself and remembering that I *am* a good person and I don't have to be perfect in every area for people to think well of me. I can start focusing on the things I want to do and stop letting other people drive the bus. I can work on having the courage of my convictions and do things the way I want to or ask for what I want (like telling Eliza I'd like to go with her to visit her family every now and then). I can tell myself that if I don't put in my best effort to all things, it's okay."

Advice

We were exhausted for Tamara, thinking about how hard she was working to manage other people's thoughts and feelings. We reminded her that people think what they think and it's rarely even close to what we imagine they are thinking or even care about.

Tamara picked the Madame Dora card "Yes, But Yolanda" who said, "Stop focusing on buts." Yolanda suggested that Tamara stop second-guessing herself and stop procrastinating. It's okay to ask for what she wants and take a stand – now!

Talk to Your Inner Child

We suggested that Tamara talk to her little kid saying, "You must be really scared and sorry. I know that feeling and you are not alone. It's okay to be feeling that. I'll be with you and I believe in you. I trust you and you are good enough."

Now It's Your Turn

To learn more about yourself, fill out the template below. Follow the instructions above to guide you. You may want to invite friends or family members to help you, especially with brainstorming when you get the sections called "Private Logic" and "Advice".

Name:_____ Date:_____

Present

Current Issue: _____

_____

Past

Childhood memory: _____

_____

_____

Private Logic:

I _____

Others _____

Life_____

Therefore _____

Future

If Nothing Changes: _____

3 A's

Awareness: _____

Acceptance: _____

Action: _____

Advice

Magic Wand: _____

Madame Dora Card: _____

Thoughts:_____

Talk to Your Inner Child:_____

_____

_____

_____

_____

Three

Kat: Struggling with Body Image

Present

Current Issue: Kat's biggest issue was her self-esteem, or as she said, her lack thereof. She described how she thought about her body as "terrible and discouraging," worried about what other people thought of her, and believed she didn't enjoy her time like most of the world does. Since she and her husband started In Vitro Fertilization (IVF) treatment to start their family, the process and hormones made huge changes in her body and emotions, including significant weight-gain. Kat felt out of control of the situation. She was not able to exercise, her usual source of emotional and physical health, not to mention an effective way of coping with stress. She said, "It's made my energy different and my lifestyle harder, so I'm being forced to accept myself as-is. I feel frustrated, worried, and stuck." Though she knew much of what she was going through was temporary, she was filled with self-doubt, and avoided looking in the mirror.

Past

Childhood Memory: Kat didn't hesitate as she let this memory surface. "I had a pool party in the fifth grade at my mom's house. A ton of my friends were there – maybe as many as ten people. It was really hot. I had on a yellow swimsuit because that was my favorite color and my hair was short, to my jaw, like a bob. Most of the girls ended up staying the night. It was super fun. I was trying to fit in, which was always a struggle for me. I felt isolated, misunderstood, uneasy, and uncomfortable.

   Kat's Private Logic: We brainstormed guesses with Kat about what the child within her had decided:

- I care a lot about how I look.

- Friends are important to me.

- I don't fit in, even though I work at it.

- I feel isolated, misunderstood, uneasy and uncomfortable.

- Others are more relaxed than I am.

- Others like to spend time with me.

- Life is about fitting in.

- Therefore I struggle be like others and to be good enough.

Future

If Nothing Changes: Kat did not want to go through life feeling isolated, misunderstood, uneasy and uncomfortable, and was concerned that was exactly where she was headed if she did not become more self-accepting.

3 A's

Awareness: Kat said that her wish to fit in was often at odds with her accepting herself the way she is. She is aware that, though her situation is temporary, she has always had the same problem with her self-image and always had the same goals and expectations for herself about looking good and fitting in.

Acceptance: Kat said, "I am someone who cares how I look to others and how I look to myself more than I care about feeling happy. I have the skills to change, but so far I haven't." She let out an unhappy sigh, frowned, took a deep breath, and then nodded. We could actually see the acceptance sinking in.

Action: Kat decided to work on being ok in the moment with how she is. "I can focus on mindfulness and routine rather than on exercise and losing weight."

Kat reflected for a moment and then said, "I try the same thing over and over expecting a different result and just end up dreary. Instead of striving for perfection, I could strive for persistence. If someone is telling me how to live, I could say, 'Fine,' and then follow my own passion and stick to it. Instead of worrying about failure, I could try new things and be okay if they don't turn out the way I thought, planned or prepared for."

Advice

We suggested that Kat try using a magic wand to encourage herself, by changing her memory or current situation in any way she wished. With a grin, she snatched the gold-painted starfish-on-a-stick we held out to her and said, "I am changing my thinking and it's a relief. Now, when I think about my future, I see a me who is fit and happy without anxiety or stress. I'm surrounded by friends and family and I'm feeling confident and comfortable getting dressed each day. I imagine going to an event and feeling good about the way I look and myself in general. Mainly, I'm not worried I'll say the wrong thing or care what people are going to think about me." This is why the wand is magic, we said. "If you can visualize something, you can create it!"

We asked Kat if she'd like some advice from the wise Madam Dora and she said, "Yes!" We handed her a deck of Madam Dora cards and without looking, she picked Courageous Cole. Cole said, "Go for it! You can do it!"

We told Kat, "Once you hold that baby in your arms, everything will change if you let it. If you allow her to teach and shape you anew, you will grow in ways you never imagined were possible for you, kind of like growing up all over again. Your whole perspective will shift."

Talk to Your Inner Child

We suggested that Kat take a walk with her inner child and talk to her the way she would talk to the new baby she'll soon hold in her arms. "You're perfect just as you are, and I love you SOOOO much!"

Now It's Your Turn

To learn more about yourself, fill out the template below. Follow the instructions above to guide you. You may want to invite friends or family members to help you, especially with brainstorming when you get the sections called "Private Logic" and "Advice".

Name:_____ Date:_____

Present

Current Issue: _____

_____

Past

Childhood memory: _____

_____

_____

Private Logic:

I _____

Others _____

Life_____

Therefore _____

Future

If Nothing Changes: _____

3 A's

Awareness: _____

Acceptance: _____

Action: _____

Advice

Magic Wand: _____

Madame Dora Card: _____

Thoughts:_____

Talk to Your Inner Child:_____

_____

_____

_____

_____

Four
Brenda: Life After Retirement

Present
Current Issue: After she retired from a lifetime in social services, Brenda moved away from the town where she'd spent decades raising her children. She moved hundreds of miles, to a city where she knew no one, because it was affordable on her small pension, and at least it was within a few hours' drive of her son, and of a dear friend. But day-to-day she felt isolated and apart within what she saw as a conservative culture. She wanted to find people with common interests and values to hers, and develop some new relationships.

She said, "The reason I loved living where I did was there were so many people like me – a community where I shared a lot of the same values with the people around me. And I don't anymore; I find that many around me have very different values and I think I have to be cautious about revealing who I really am."

Past
Childhood Memory: Brenda could not access a childhood memory. She blanked. Sometimes that happens. It's ok to use something in the more recent past if that's all you have. It works just as well. Here's what Brenda shared: "It's maybe a year ago, and I'm taking my daily after-work walk with my friend Beverly and our two dogs. We're talking about our day, laughing a lot, like every other block! I feel calm, light, and healthy."

Brenda's Private Logic: We made these guesses about Brenda's private logic:

- I can talk about anything.

- I bond with people like me.

- Others share my interests and values.

- Life is a place where I can laugh and exercise with a kindred soul.

- Therefore I'm relaxed, uninhibited and sharing what comes to mind.

Currently her life doesn't match these at all, and she's unhappy. The distance between a person's belief about how life should be and how it actually is, is called *stress*. Right now Brenda is pretty stressed by what she sees as the cultural divide between her and the rest of her new community.

Her son recently married a woman who is deeply religious, and who conforms with her church's teaching that homosexuality is unnatural and sinful. Though he was raised with deeply-held humanist values in Brenda's household, her son is now converting to his wife's religion. Brenda now feels at risk of alienating her son, his wife, and their children if she is outspoken about her disagreements with their religion.

Future
If nothing changes, Brenda's future will be one of loneliness and isolation. Her fear is that, if she is open about who she really is, not only will there be no close friendships in her new community, but it will be difficult to be herself even with her son, his wife, and her grandchildren.

3 A's
Awareness: Brenda said that the reason she loved living where she did

was that there were so many people like her – a community where we shared a lot of the same values. "And I don't anymore, I find that many around me have very different values and I am cautious about revealing who I really am."

Acceptance: Brenda said, "I'm more comfortable with people who think like I do and have the same values. It's with them that I feel free and happy. But I do live in a community and have close family members who, with their religion, are 'of a different culture' than I am. I do not want to lie about who I am because it's really uncomfortable."

Action: Thinking about what baby steps she could take, Brenda said, "Maybe my standards are too rigid, my circle too small. I may have to venture out of my surroundings in order to make happen what I want for me. The Woman's March was my happiest day other than those with family or friends. It was rewarding. I was not by myself. There was a big community out there but they didn't come from my town; I can get involved there."

Advice

We had a few ideas for Brenda, too: Look beyond the either/or: Find the in-between. Post on Facebook or the March Site looking for kindred spirits nearby you. Start or join a group: a play group, women's group, activist group branch.

Brenda picked a Madame Dora card for another perspective on her problem and she pulled Discerning Darla. When she began to read Darla's advice, she breathed a sigh of relief when she read, "Whether it comes in the form of a person or a project, it's not what it appears to be at first glance. Be discerning. Look for the profound and you'll find it, and that will make all the difference in the near future."

Now It's Your Turn

To learn more about yourself, fill out the template below. Follow the instructions above to guide you. You may want to invite friends or family members to help you, especially with brainstorming when you get the sections called "Private Logic" and "Advice".

Name:_____ Date:_____

Present

Current Issue: _____

_____

Past

Childhood memory: _____

_____

_____

Private Logic:

I _____

Others _____

Life_____

Therefore _____

Future

If Nothing Changes: _____

3 A's

Awareness: _____

Acceptance: _____

Action: _____

Advice

Magic Wand: _____

Madame Dora Card: _____

Thoughts:_____

Talk to Your Inner Child:_____

_____

_____

_____

_____

Five
Molly: Breaking Up with Work Partners

Present

Current Issue: Molly has been going through a painful breakup with two work partners. Even though they parted on good terms, later Molly thought she had been betrayed and felt hurt. She decided not to partner with the two again.

Past

Childhood Memory: Molly remembered that when she was a young girl in her little village, she had two good friends. As young girls often do, Minmin, Nini and Molly took turns becoming each other's best friends. It seemed there were always just two who were the best friends. Best friends talked about many things, including gossiping about the third one. Molly always thought Minmin was her best friend, although they fought a lot. One day Molly realized that Nini and Minmin were closer, and that Minmin and Molly had stopped talking. Later Minmin and her family moved away.

When Molly became a teenager, Minmin moved back to Molly's village, but they still didn't talk to each other. If they passed each other on the street, they pretended they did not see each other. Even after Molly went away to college, when she came back to visit her hometown she still could not bring herself to chat naturally or even say a proper "Hi" to Minmin.

When she went back to her memory, she saw herself in the alleys or the classrooms, sitting melancholy in her seat, wandering in silence, feeling abandoned and lonely, all the while thinking that her two friends were saying nasty things about her. She had believed that when the three of them told each other that they would always be good friends, they would keep their word. Otherwise, it would be a betrayal. Once the girls failed to keep their promises, Molly took it personally and decided that they were untrustworthy and immoral.

Molly's Private Logic: When this memory hit Molly out of the blue, she almost burst into tears. She had not known she was still hurt from such a betrayal of trust. And she came to understand her private logic better and how it was influencing her life in the present. Here are some guesses we made about Molly's private logic:

- I put my trust in others.

- Others should be trustworthy and keep their promises.

- Life is a place where others betray my trust.

- Therefore, I "break up" with others.

Future
If Nothing Changes: Molly didn't realize how troubled her adult life was because of her childhood decisions. She remembered cutting off a relationship she had with a close friend and colleague when the colleague started missing appointments and not returning phone calls. They didn't speak for two years. Molly understood that, if nothing changed, her beliefs would cost her many future valuable allies and relationships. She was worried that no one would like her and that she would be without support or friends.

The 3 A's
Awareness: Molly was aware of how her thinking had become very black or white, that she demanded 100% commitment to a relationship,

blind loyalty and nothing going awry, and that by not putting up with anything less, she was the most moral person and better than others. Molly's awareness of her pattern of cutting people off left her with a strong desire to change.

Acceptance: She accepted that she was hurt and lonely, believing she had been wronged and betrayed.

Action: Her awareness and acceptance gave Molly the courage to take action. She thought of some baby steps she knew she could take. She also decided that she would count her blessings every day before she got out of bed. She reminded herself that she had a great marriage, one beautiful kid and a loving husband, and that she was beautiful inside and out.

Advice
Our advice to Molly was to draw a Madame Dora card in the morning and focus on the message while she brushed her teeth. The card she pulled was *Wise Walter,* who said, "Don't make problems you don't have." Molly laughed and said, "Well, I didn't expect that, but it's really helpful advice which I will take seriously."

Talk to Your Inner Child
Molly pretended she had a magic wand and could go back and talk to her six-year-old self and encourage her. She imagined sitting next to her on the couch, saying, "You were afraid no one would like you and that you wouldn't have friends. I love you for who you are and I will always be with you." Molly felt understood and relieved and she wept.

Now It's Your Turn

To learn more about yourself, fill out the template below. Follow the instructions above to guide you. You may want to invite friends or family members to help you, especially with brainstorming when you get the sections called "Private Logic" and "Advice".

Name:_____ Date:_____

Present

Current Issue: _____

_____

Past

Childhood memory: _____

_____

_____

Private Logic:

I _____

Others _____

Life_____

Therefore _____

Future

If Nothing Changes: _____

3 A's

Awareness: _____

Acceptance: _____

Action: _____

Advice

Magic Wand: _____

Madame Dora Card:_____

Thoughts:_____

Talk to Your Inner Child:_____

_____

_____

_____

_____

Six

Annie: Should We Get Divorced?

Present

Current Issue: Annie was brought up short when her husband threatened to leave her because she was spending virtually no time with him. She was surprised and terrified. She loves her husband and doesn't want to lose him. Thinking about what he said, she realized she had been in a familiar pattern at work where once she gets involved in a project, it's all she can think about and she spends all her time on it, ignoring everything else. She said, "I just get too busy and can't stop." Annie understood that her old pattern was threatening to destroy her marriage.

Past

Childhood Memory: Annie thought of a childhood memory and wrote it down. She remembered when she was three or four years old and was playing with a boy at the playground. She was pretending to be a princess and wanted that boy to watch her as she played. Although the memory seemed unrelated to her current situation, Annie trusted that it had come to her mind because it would offer some insight into her private logic.

Annie's Private Logic: We made some guesses about how the three-year-old inside her was coaching her about being in a relationship with a male:

- If I act like a princess, the boy's job is to watch me.

- I play while others watch.

- Boys (men) should watch me, enthralled and admiring.

- When I am busy and active, others focus on me.

- Life is a place where I am busy and engaged and others take their cues from me.

- Therefore, I stay busy and expect others to watch and cheer.

Annie's face lit up and she agreed. "I never realized before that I do need to have my own pattern and I need others to follow it. In fact, my husband and I had an argument recently because he complained that, not only am I too busy traveling, but that when I am home, I'm not really present, not there for him. When he said that, I felt angry and sad because I thought that was his way of saying he doesn't love me anymore. I finally asked him if he feels lonely when I'm not home, and he smiled and said yes. I never realized that I expect and even need him to treat me like a princess, watching me play around, and to say 'You did a great job and I still love you even though you're busy.'"

Future
If Nothing Changes: Annie reflected that if nothing changes, in the future she could see that she and her husband would spend more time quarrelling when they are together, and he might end up leaving the marriage.

3 A's
We followed up our work together by asking Annie to share her three A's. Here's what she shared:

Awareness: "I'm aware that sometimes I like to be a princess and the feeling is good."

Acceptance: "I accept that it's okay to be a princess, but not all the time."

Action: "My action will be to talk about what I am learning about myself with my husband."

Advice

We suggested that Annie make plans with her husband to regularly spend Special Time together. What makes Special Time special is that it is planned, regular and a commitment that you keep. It's one thing to talk about spending time together, but the truth is in the doing. It's one thing to make a promise, but it's another to follow through with action. We suggested that Annie get some advice from the Madame Dora cards to help her upgrade her private logic. Without looking, she picked Strong Simon from the deck. His message is, "Hold on. You're almost there."

Annie said, "To me this means that I'm moving in the right direction. I think I got this card because my husband and I are both trying really hard to create a new pattern. I think we can move in the right direction by scheduling special time together each week."

Talk to Your Inner Child

Annie talks to her 4-year old inner child: "You must be feeling very happy and proud to be a pretend princess and having the boy watching you. I would have loved that too. Little girls just love that and it is all right. Do you want me to take beautiful pictures so that you can always be a princess like this?"

Now It's Your Turn

To learn more about yourself, fill out the template below. Follow the instructions above to guide you. You may want to invite friends or family members to help you, especially with brainstorming when you get the sections called "Private Logic" and "Advice".

Name:_____ Date:_____

Present

Current Issue: _____

_____

Past

Childhood memory: _____

_____

_____

Private Logic:

I _____

Others _____

Life_____

Therefore _____

Future

If Nothing Changes: _____

3 A's

Awareness: _____

Acceptance: _____

Action: _____

Advice

Magic Wand: _____

Madame Dora Card: _____

Thoughts:_____

Talk to Your Inner Child:_____

_____

_____

_____

_____

Seven
Sheryl: Power Struggle with Work Colleague

Present

Current Issue: Sheryl was having conflicts with her colleague Amber. Describing a recent company meeting where they were discussing how to promote trainings, she told us, "Amber complained that I didn't describe what goes on each flyer accurately. She was frustrated with me, and she snapped, 'I need details!'"

Sheryl continued, "We are very different. Sometimes I push her too much, give her too much information or ask for too much help, and she gets stressed out. It drives her crazy when I'm not clear, although the flyers were clear in my mind."

Past

Childhood Memory: We asked Sheryl to let a specific memory from her childhood come to mind, even if it seemed unrelated to the current issue. She said, "I was 4 or 5 years old and living with my grandma in the countryside in a village, just the two of us. My parents and my siblings were in the city. My grandma raised chickens. We didn't have our own farm because I was too young and Grandma was too old. In the memory, I am carrying a blanket to neighborhood farms to collect rice to feed our chickens. After the harvest there is still lots of rice left. All the land is very flat and huge, with different parts owned by different people, but I'm free to collect. The rice is golden. I feel happy and safe and free because I can do what I want. I feel capable because I can help Grandma and the chickens."

Sheryl's Private Logic: From Sheryl's memory, we made some guesses about the beliefs she formed as a child that may still govern her life and shape her reality as an adult:

- I am capable.

- I work by myself to help others.

- I can do what I want.

- Others need my help and appreciate it.

- Others trust me to help.

- Life is challenging, but I am up to the task.

- Therefore, I need to work hard to contribute.

Future
If Nothing Changes: Sheryl said, "I will keep working to be the one to 'feed our chickens', and Amber and I will continue to have conflicts. She will not appreciate or trust my help and I will not be able to contribute. Both of us will feel miserable, and miss out on the harvest!"

At this point, Sheryl's eyes were getting shiny with tears. Shaking her head, she shared a dream of the future she wished for: "If we trust each other to do our part, we'll have a harvest. We'll both work hard. We'll have lots of self-reflection, discussion and improvement. We'll balance our family, enjoy our lives and do our work while we are still learning, working and exploring. Like the golden picture! Instead of me feeding our chickens, together Amber and I will be helping more kids and families, and saving the world one by one."

3 A's

Awareness: Sheryl said, "I act like I still have to work alone to take care of others who need my help."

Acceptance: "When I think others need my help, my inner child takes over."

Action: "I will do better by talking less, not overwhelming others with information. I could focus on keeping my sentences to 10 words or less."

Advice

Madame Dora had some thoughts to offer Sheryl. Sheryl drew Open-Minded Ophelia, who said, "You are looking too hard for a mirror image of yourself. You're judging others by narrow standards that keep you unhappy and lonely. A surprise relationship is just around the corner. You'll discover new happiness with a person (Amber) you previously judged harshly and wrongly."

We had these thoughts to add for Sheryl: "You are like a rock and clear in your heart. Others question things more. You asked Amber to join you. You don't doubt yourself. You are the person with eyes and she's the person with legs. If you can help her see your vision, she can work with you to make both of your dreams come true."

Talk to Your Inner Child

Sheryl knows what to say to her inner child: "The harvest is golden, the land is flat, and you are free to collect. It is such a wonderful life you are having. You are able and capable, and you love freedom so much. To do what you want is important to you, and to help makes you feel capable. I understand you better now."

Now It's Your Turn

To learn more about yourself, fill out the template below. Follow the instructions above to guide you. You may want to invite friends or family members to help you, especially with brainstorming when you get the sections called "Private Logic" and "Advice".

Name:_____ Date:_____

Present

Current Issue: _____

_____

Past

Childhood memory: _____

_____

_____

Private Logic:

I _____

Others _____

Life_____

Therefore _____

Future

If Nothing Changes: _____

3 A's

Awareness: _____

Acceptance: _____

Action: _____

Advice

Magic Wand: _____

Madame Dora Card:_____

Thoughts:_____

Talk to Your Inner Child:_____

_____

_____

_____

_____

Eight

Kathy: The Cost of Micromanaging

Present

Current Issue: Kathy was frustrated because people were letting her down and she decided she couldn't rely on other people. She knew this was counter-productive, because she was starting a new business, and there was no way she could possibly do everything herself.

Past

Childhood Memory: Kathy shared the following: "I remember when I was 5 years old. I'm playing with my mom and dad and sister and it's a rare thing that we're all in the same room together. Dad is rough housing with my sister and me and Mom is laughing. Suddenly Dad roles over and his arm lands on our doll crib and he breaks the crib.

He looks really downcast and angry with himself. He stops wrestling with us, gets mad at himself and leaves the room. I felt happy and excited when we were playing and felt surprised because that was such a rare thing. When he broke the crib I felt angry and disappointed and frustrated and kind of despairing. Even at that young age I remember thinking that everything good goes away and that I can't trust that things are the way I want them to be and I can't rely on other people."

Kathy's Private Logic: Here are our guesses about Kathy's private logic:

- I can't rely on other people.

- I am happy when people are nice, but get scared and disappointed when people change.

- Others are inconsistent and sometimes even scary.

- Others should control themselves and behave.

- Life is a place where everything good goes away, where I can't get help and support from others, and where the best I can do is to do things myself, and do them for others.

- Therefore, I have to be the one who is consistent, reliable, really good, gets things done and doing things for others.

Future

If Nothing Changes: Kathy said, "I realize I've carried these beliefs with me my entire life. If I don't make any changes in the future, I'll probably end up working really hard, having to be good all the time, getting walked all over and feeling bad about myself because now I really know better."

3 A's

Awareness: Kathy said, "Doing this activity has really helped me be aware of how much I work too hard trying to control relationships."

Acceptance: Kathy realized that she was really angry with others who allow her to micro-manage everything, and she was angry with herself as well because she ignores her feelings and wants while trying to be a hero to everyone else.

Action: Kathy decided that she could relax and trust other people to do the work. Instead of micro-managing, she could notice her feelings about people's behavior and maybe even talk it over with them.

Advice

Kathy decided to draw two Madame Dora cards. The advice Trusting Tilly and Genuine Ginny gave her was that she doesn't need to manage relationships or try to control the future. What she does need to do is to live in the now with the way things are and trust that they'll work out. Genuine Ginny also told her to stop acting like a hero so people would like her, because people will love her for who she is, not for who she wants them to think she is.

Talk to Your Inner Child
We suggested to Kathy that she pretend her 5-year-old inner child was right in front of her, and that she tell her, "You didn't do anything wrong. You didn't make this happen. You can't change him no matter how hard you try. It's okay to play on your own and let him calm himself down."

Now It's Your Turn

To learn more about yourself, fill out the template below. Follow the instructions above to guide you. You may want to invite friends or family members to help you, especially with brainstorming when you get the sections called "Private Logic" and "Advice".

Name:_____ Date:_____

Present

Current Issue: _____
_____

Past

Childhood memory: _____
_____
_____

Private Logic:

I _____

Others _____

Life_____

Therefore _____

Future

If Nothing Changes: _____

3 A's

Awareness: _____

Acceptance: _____

Action: _____

Advice

Magic Wand: _____

Madame Dora Card:_____

Thoughts:_____

Talk to Your Inner Child:_____
_____
_____
_____
_____

Nine

Karen: Learning to be Encouraging to Yourself and Others

Present

Current Issue: Karen and two of her colleagues completed teaching a parenting class together. They had an agreement that when the class was completed, one of the co-teachers would write an article summarizing the benefits of the class to promote future work. When a month had gone by and the article had not been written, Karen said, "What, you didn't finish yet? It's a month late!"

As soon as the words came out of her mouth, Karen realized that though she'd decided to be more encouraging, she was not following through. She wondered what private logic was getting in her way?

Past

Childhood Memory: Here's the memory she came up with. "When I was three or four, like most children in China at that time, I lived with my grandparents. My grandfather was sick and just sat on the bed while I played nearby on the floor. My Auntie, who was my grandparents' youngest daughter, lived with us. She was maybe 20 years old, and was trying to teach me a Chinese poem, but I just couldn't remember it. My grandfather got impatient and scolded her, saying, "Stop trying to teach her. She is stupid!" When I heard this, I thought my grandfather didn't like me. I felt sad and lonely, and decided that he was right that I was stupid and couldn't learn anything.

Karen's Private Logic: If we guess what her private logic might be, it would sound something like this:

- I am stupid and can't do the right thing.

- Others have the right to judge me.

- Life is a test of competence where I don't measure up.

- Therefore, there's no point in trying.

Future

If Nothing Changes: Even though Karen had decided to be more encouraging, when she felt upset, she fell back on talking to others the way she had been talked to as a child. She knew it was discouraging to both her and others to talk that way.

3 A's
Awareness: Karen's biggest ah-hah was that she started letting others define her when she was very young. She has carried that behavior with her into adulthood, judging others as she was judged as a child.

Acceptance: Though it was difficult to admit to herself, she realized how discouraging she had become like the adults in her childhood were to her.

Action: Karen has learned many new skills as an adult. One of the most helpful was to notice her feelings and to name them. Even though she may not be able to do this in a moment of upset or confrontation (hardly anyone can do that!), she decided that when she is calmer, she can name her feeling and express it to herself and others.

Advice
Karen decided to pick a Madame Dora card for help. She drew "Mature Matilda." Matilda advised, "Stop taking everything personally." Karen acknowledged that was useful advice. It takes time to realize that what people say is more about themselves than about the person they are talking to. With her new awareness, Karen could go back to her colleague with the courage to simply say how she felt when her colleague didn't keep her promise about writing and publishing the article. She

knows she will feel better by telling her colleague her thoughts and feelings and that she will do better by waiting until she is calmer to have that conversation.

Our recommendation to Karen is to remember that it is okay to have feelings and, instead of judging them, she can learn to name them. One of our colleagues talks about doing three things with feelings – name them, claim them and aim them. For Karen, naming her feelings would be angry and disappointed and let down. Claiming them would be admitting to herself it is how she feels. Aiming them would be what we suggested Karen could do in the Advice section – share her thoughts and feelings with her colleagues when she feels calm.

Talk to Your Inner Child

Karen might say to her inner child, "You do not need to believe what your grandpa said. It is only natural for kids to take time to memorize a poem, and it is natural that you cannot learn it in a day. You are like every child and you are unique. Believe in yourself."

Now It's Your Turn

To learn more about yourself, fill out the template below. Follow the instructions above to guide you. You may want to invite friends or family members to help you, especially with brainstorming when you get the sections called "Private Logic" and "Advice".

Name:_____ Date:_____

Present

Current Issue: _____

_____

Past

Childhood memory: _____

_____

_____

Private Logic:

I _____

Others _____

Life_____

Therefore _____

Future

If Nothing Changes: _____

3 A's

Awareness: _____

Acceptance: _____

Action: _____

Advice

Magic Wand: _____

Madame Dora Card: _____

Thoughts:_____

Talk to Your Inner Child:_____

_____

_____

_____

_____

Ten

Harley: Dealing with Feelings of Embarrassment and Shame

Present

Current Issue: How do I want to spend my time productively?

Past

Childhood Memory: Harley said, "I am at Scout Camp (8-9 years old). I'm on one side of this creek / waterway / whatever it is. Most of the kids can jump across it without any problem, and when I try to jump, I land in the water. I didn't really try that hard – I held myself back and ended in the water. I felt embarrassed and inadequate."

Harley's Private Logic: We brainstormed together with Harley, and came up with the following list of guesses about the beliefs he formed as an eight-year-old that are still operating today:

- I don't really try that hard.

- I hold myself back because I'm scared.

- I let myself down by not trying hard enough.

- I can't succeed because I think I'll make mistakes.

- I feel embarrassed if I'm not immediately successful.

- I believe I'm inadequate which stops me from trying new things and learning from experience

- I think if I'm not already perfect, I shouldn't bother trying because I'll only embarrass myself and feel inadequate.

- Others can succeed without any problem.

- Life is a place where the way forward is to jump; it is a challenge and a contest that I can't win.

- Therefore, I don't try very hard and end up in the water. I've already decided I can't do it so I give up before I start.

Future

If Nothing Changes: Harley said, "I'll continue to give up before I start because I've already decided I can't do it so why even try."

3 A's

Awareness: Harley's expression grew sad with his realization. "I'm used to doing the things that I can do well or perfectly right from the start. The minute I have any trouble, I don't bother to try or learn by doing."

Acceptance: Thinking back on his life, Harley realized how much he'd stuck with doing what came easily for him and how quickly he'd given up when something was difficult.

Action: Harley realized that he had to get in and try something to see how it would work for him to know if it was something he really wanted to do. "Once I've tried as hard as I can at a thing I may be interested in, I need to trust my feelings and either move forward with it or just move on."

Advice

With a grin, Harley rummaged among the Madame Dora cards and pulled out "Courageous Cole" whose advice was, "Try again!"

He also chose a tool card from the parenting deck, which turned out to be "letting go". He said, "I would tell the little kid in me to let go of the idea that you have to compete to be like the others. I would say, just go out there and try to do the best that is you."

If we compare ourselves to others or some perceived "should," we can be pretty sure to stop ourselves from ever trying. Feelings of embarrassment and shame are about "shoulds". It's part of the human condition to make mistakes, so instead of comparing yourself to others, if you make a mistake, try again!

Talk to Your Inner Child

Harley is quite experienced in talking to his inner child. He said, "You must have believed you couldn't make it to the other side and felt ashamed. Be yourself and you will shine in your own ways."

Now It's Your Turn

To learn more about yourself, fill out the template below. Follow the instructions above to guide you. You may want to invite friends or family members to help you, especially with brainstorming when you get the sections called "Private Logic" and "Advice".

Name:_____ Date:_____

Present

Current Issue: _____

_____

Past

Childhood memory: _____

_____

_____

Private Logic:

I _____

Others _____

Life_____

Therefore _____

Future

If Nothing Changes: _____

3 A's

Awareness: _____

Acceptance: _____

Action: _____

Advice

Magic Wand: _____

Madame Dora Card:_____

Thoughts:_____

Talk to Your Inner Child:_____

_____

_____

_____

_____

Eleven

Rudi: Am I Ready for Parenthood?

Present

Current Issue: When Rudi learned Kerry was actually pregnant and they heard the heartbeat, he was excited after all they'd had to go through. He is happy but also worried that what they'd wanted so much is now not just a thought, but a living being. He wants to be able to be a father while still having and doing what he wishes. He is concerned it could be a conflict because he wants enough income to have certain things like a car, home, school, but also wants the freedom to do the activities – particularly outdoors – that require free time, rather than money. He is feeling conflicted and doubtful that he will be able to have both.

Past

Childhood Memory: Rudi recalled, "I was a young teenager and my dad and I went backpacking in Trinity and then to the "Hog Farm Pignick" after that. I had a sense of freedom experiencing the best of fun and freedom in both worlds: being outdoors but then having fun at the festival. I felt free, not tied down, happy, and free of responsibility."

Rudi's Private Logic: Rudi's memory depicts his idea of "how life should be". Here are our guesses about Rudi's private logic:

- I want a lot of freedom and fun.

- I don't want to have to choose between freedom and responsibility.

- Others (like my dad) introduce me to a world of fun and I love sharing it together.

- Life is best when fun and freedom are combined, especially outdoors.

- Therefore I join with others to pursue that fun and freedom.

Future
If Nothing Changes: Rudi said, "I can't imagine Kerry and me and our child living in a country spot surrounded by forest in a house with no fence, feeling happy and not burdened with worries, even though that's what I want."

3A's
Awareness: Like most anyone facing parenthood for the first time, Rudi is keenly aware of his mixed feelings. His high regard for freedom, he says, seems counterintuitive to wanting a child. He thinks that in some ways, having a child is liberating. "I could bring the kid with me," he says, and adds that that could be so enjoyable for him that including the child would not seem burdensome. At the same time, he has a sense of having no control over what happens in the future in his life, "… starting with whether it's a boy or girl and whether the kid is going to do what it wants to do and be my teacher or do what I want to do."

Acceptance: Rudi acknowledges that his biggest challenge may be staying present. "I want to tell myself that things will be okay. Things will be good, even when they are tough."

Action: Rudi says he intends to focus on being present and not trying to juggle too many things or people at once. "Being present will help me to see and notice those good things daily. I can focus on slowing down a little and living more simply, creating time in my day to have stillness and quiet, and time to reflect."

Advice
The Madame Dora card Rudi drew was Trusting Tilly, who said, "Everything is ok. If you're asking about the future, I can guarantee that in the long run everything works out if you concentrate on how you live your life today." How apt is that?

We suggested that Rudi realize that he is exactly where he needs to be. We reminded him that he's not alone in the concerns and questions he's raising for himself. Even as they're central to who he is, we reminded him that his concerns are common, one way or another, with just about every parent-to-be and that he will be a well-connected kind of parent. We believe he will strike the balance needed without compromising who he is while still providing leadership and guidance to his child.

Talk to Your Inner Child

Tell him, "Someday you'll be a father and you'll get to share your love of the outdoors with your own kids. They will be so lucky to get to have adventures with you."

Now It's Your Turn

To learn more about yourself, fill out the template below. Follow the instructions above to guide you. You may want to invite friends or family members to help you, especially with brainstorming when you get the sections called "Private Logic" and "Advice".

Name:_____ Date:_____

Present

Current Issue: _____

_____

Past

Childhood memory: _____

_____

_____

Private Logic:

I _____

Others _____

Life_____

Therefore _____

Future

If Nothing Changes: _____

3 A's

Awareness: _____

Acceptance: _____

Action: _____

Advice

Magic Wand: _____

Madame Dora Card: _____

Thoughts:_____

Talk to Your Inner Child:_____

_____

_____

_____

_____

Twelve
Rory: Am I Losing Mental Capacity?

Present

Current Issue: In his mid-sixties, Rory was having trouble remembering things – especially for work. He said, "I'm always wondering if I've done everything that I need to do, having to go back and double-check if I've done something or not." He was feeling frightened and concerned that he was losing his mental capacity. He also said he felt angry that it creates so much more work for him because he needs to make extensive notes and lists, then double-check the lists to make sure they're all accurate. This behavior exponentially increases his workload because he thinks he has to repeat everything.

He gave us some examples. "In a teleconference, I'll be trying to get information from attendees, but I can't remember if I've already asked for it in the meeting or gathered it before. Or I'll be making out a schedule and get anxious because I've forgotten if I've already scheduled something on a certain date and then somehow double-booked. I feel embarrassed, angry, and resentful of the additional hassle."

Past

Childhood Memory: What first came vividly to mind for Rory was actually a memory from just ten years earlier. He shared, "My dad lost a lot of his mental capacity before he died. He didn't remember where he parked his car one time when he went to the store

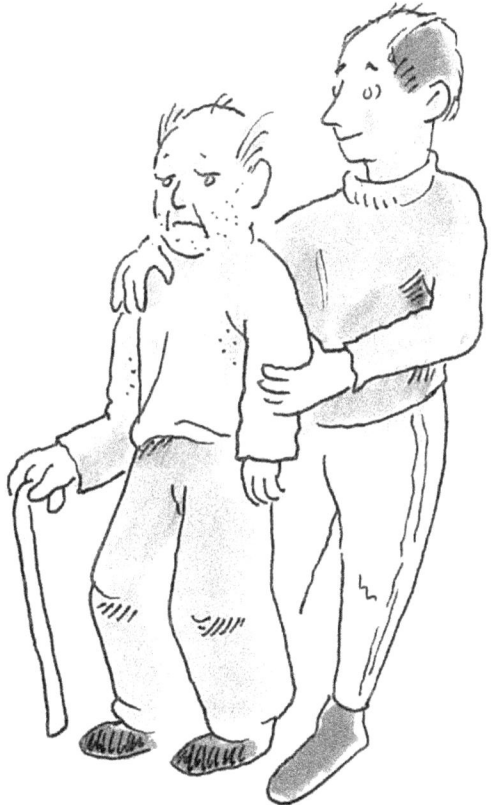

and was wandering around town until a neighbor spotted him, asked if he was okay and brought him home. I heard about this from both parents, and as I listened, I felt really bad for my dad, really sad and concerned. I thought, 'He's losing his independence and it's going to be a change in lifestyle for him. Probably he won't be able to drive or go out on his own anymore.'"

Rory's Private Logic: We brainstormed guesses with Rory about what he had decided:

- I feel empathy for others.

- I see their life change as they get older in ways they won't like and can't fix.

- Others look out for them as they become more and more dependent.

- Life is a place where aging comes with a lot of loss, and changes we don't like and can't fix.

- Life is a place where others look out for us and we lose our independence.

- Therefore I worry this is already happening to me.

Future
If Nothing Changes: Rory is concerned he will not be able to do his job because of the mistakes he makes. He said, "I don't have a system or the wherewithal to juggle all these balls at once. I've double-booked someone and have to decide who I'm going to break the news that the schedule doesn't work anymore, apologize for the mistake, and then start from square one again. I feel angry, resentful, and embarrassed. On a deeper level, I'm wondering if I'm suited for this job anymore."

3 A's
Awareness: Rory said, "I'm aware that I'm worried, maybe even a little scared, of aging, in case these mental changes that can come with aging are something that happens in my family and may already be happening to me."

Acceptance: Acknowledging that others had not complained or pointed out any of the mistakes that had been concerning him, Rory said, "It may not be a problem for anyone else because I haven't gotten any feedback that says that." But it is a problem for him, as he spends enormous time and energy developing and using mnemonics and reminder lists he never had to use before.

Action: Rory is already adopting new behaviors to cope with the challenges: making sure he gets plenty of sleep, avoiding alcohol during the week, and managing stress by working out regularly. He reminds himself it will be just another year until he retires and he thinks he can "tough it out" till then.

Advice

We suggested that Rory pretend he had a magic wand to wave over this situation. What would he change? He said, "It's less busy! That would be perfect!"

We had a final suggestion: Rory could retire *now*. Or he could get tested for what he fears might be happening in his brain. He could also ask others for a reality check.

Talk to Your Inner Child

We also asked Rory what he would say to his inner child about what is going on and he replied, "When you were a kid, you thought life as it was would go on forever. Now that you're an adult, you know that both life and people change and there's no way around it. Seize the day!"

Now It's Your Turn

To learn more about yourself, fill out the template below. Follow the instructions above to guide you. You may want to invite friends or family members to help you, especially with brainstorming when you get the sections called "Private Logic" and "Advice".

Name:_____ Date:_____

Present

Current Issue: _____

_____

Past

Childhood memory: _____

_____

_____

Private Logic:

I _____

Others _____

Life_____

Therefore _____

Future

If Nothing Changes: _____

3 A's

Awareness: _____

Acceptance: _____

Action: _____

Advice

Magic Wand: _____

Madame Dora Card: _____

Thoughts:_____

Talk to Your Inner Child:_____

_____

_____

_____

_____

Thirteen
Margaret: Unexpected Work Change

Present

Current Issue: Margaret told us that this interview was very timely for her because her church was in the process of deciding to change their focus on marriage and family. Margaret and her husband Greg have worked with families for thirty years doing spiritual counseling and this change would certainly affect their work, though she wasn't sure how.

Past

Childhood Memory: Margaret was quick to share a memory from when she was eight to ten years old. In the memory, she was coming home from a bike ride with her sister and her mother met the two girls at the door saying their turtle had walked away. Margaret felt puzzled and surprised and thought, "How does a turtle walk away?"

Margaret's Private Logic: We made guesses as to Margaret's private logic based on her memory. Margaret is active; Margaret likes spending time with a companion; Margaret has strong views about right and wrong and possible and impossible; Margaret questions things she considers irrational. Putting private logic into categories of I, Others, Life and Therefore based on the memory might sound like the following for Margaret:

- I am logical, active and a companion.

- Others enjoy being with me.

- Others aren't always clear and logical.

- Life is predictable, and when it isn't, it's a surprise.

- Therefore, I try to puzzle out discrepancies by myself.

Margaret was quick to make the connection between her memory and her current situation. The situation with the church was surprising and puzzling to her. She wondered how the church could walk away from spiritual counseling and parent education. As she thought about it more, she wondered if the church had already changed directions and that was why she and Greg hadn't gotten a referral for months. She and Greg were operating under the assumption that nothing had changed. They had even trained two couples and were recruiting more people who could be involved with spiritual counseling. Margaret didn't ask her questions out loud, but she was clear that what was going on with the church was wrong and being handled poorly.

True to form, when deciding what to do about the situation, Margaret honored her sense of responsibility and hoped that things would work out. She didn't discuss this with either the church or another couple who they would like to work with. She said, "Greg and I aren't ready to say forget it to the church or spiritual counseling, so we have to find a path as we go forward that includes both."

3 A's

Awareness: Margaret said, "I'm aware that I'm *not* aware of all the things people think and feel and especially the decision maker's vision."

Acceptance: Margaret's comment was, "It is what it is, but as I think back over my life, I have trouble accepting that when the leadership decides something, they don't always make people aware of what's going on."

Action: Margaret was clear about what her action would be. She would quit taking things personally and she would stop internalizing her thoughts and feelings and blaming herself. Instead, she decided to lighten up and accept what's coming, and she would share her thoughts and feelings with others. She chuckled and said, "That's advice I give lots of people." Then, with a big ah hah of recognition, Margaret said, "Wow, I'm doing what I dislike from others. I'm keeping my thoughts, feelings and opinions to myself."

Advice

Thinking about what Margaret experienced, we are reminded that what happens in our life impacts us and we have feelings about it, but we didn't cause it and it's not our fault. Sometimes it's too easy to blame yourself or to feel sorry for yourself or believe you are a victim. You have lots of action choices in your situation.

We encouraged Margaret that when she feels stuck in a life situation and can't think of an action to take, she can get inspiration in four different ways.

- She can pretend she has a magic wand that she can wave over the situation and change it. That will give her a clear picture of how she would like life to be, which is very helpful to hold on to.

- She can use the Dora Advice cards and pull a card without peeking to get advice from one of the Advisors. Just knowing that there are options can be freeing.

- Or she could ask another person what they would do in her situation. Again, it helps to be aware of other perspectives and private logic decisions to ponder.

- Finally, she can accept that life isn't the way she thinks it should be and decide how she will handle the disappointment.

Talk to Your Inner Child

We also asked Margaret what she would say to her inner child about what is going on and she replied, "It doesn't make a difference how the turtle disappeared. You loved your turtle and now it's gone. I'm so very sorry. Maybe at some future time, you might want to think about getting a new pet. I'll be here to help you."

Now It's Your Turn

To learn more about yourself, fill out the template below. Follow the instructions above to guide you. You may want to invite friends or family members to help you, especially with brainstorming when you get the sections called "Private Logic" and "Advice".

Name:_____ Date:_____

Present

Current Issue: _____
_____

Past

Childhood memory: _____
_____
_____

Private Logic:

I _____

Others _____

Life_____

Therefore _____

Future

If Nothing Changes: _____

3 A's

Awareness: _____

Acceptance: _____

Action: _____

Advice

Magic Wand: _____

Madame Dora Card: _____

Thoughts:_____

Talk to Your Inner Child:_____
_____
_____
_____
_____

Fourteen

Gina: Waiting for Mr. Right

Present

Current Issue: Gina said she found dating to be a pain – difficult and a waste of time. When she thought about her past experiences, she decided to forget about dating. This, unfortunately, conflicted with her goal to be part of a loving partnership.

Past

Childhood Memory: To find out what private logic might be at work supporting her problem, we asked Gina to think of the first memory from her childhood that came to her mind, and to describe how old she was, what happened, and how she felt. She asked if she should think back to her first dating experience, and we explained that, since she already had in mind the issue she wanted help with, all she needed to do was to allow *any* memory to surface and tell it to us. Even if the memory wasn't about dating, it would help her understand her private logic. Here's what came to her:

"When I was maybe four, there was a big, big storm. After it was over, I rode on my dad's shoulders around the neighborhood, looking at all the trees that were down, and he was talking to the neighbors. It was fun and I felt happy."

Gina's Private Logic: Many people have memories that reveal their private logic about "how life should be". This one of Gina's is a good example. These are the guesses we made about her beliefs, based on the memory she shared:

- I don't have to worry about anything.

- I'm happy when I'm above it all.

- Others carry me.

- Others do the work, assessing the damage.

- Life should be fun and safe – a place where storms and damage are far from me.

- Therefore I expect others to deal with the damage.

Future
If Nothing Changes: If Gina continues through life operating from this logic, how might this impact her ability to have a loving relationship? She might find someone who is temporarily willing to deal with all the problems that come up, but it's probably not a recipe for a long-term loving relationship.

3 A's
Awareness: With a rueful smile, Gina acknowledged that she's a person who doesn't want to "do stuff" to have what she wants. She just wants it to be fun and easy and let others figure things out and do the work.

Acceptance: Gina said. "The truth is, I really prefer not to have to work at finding a relationship."

Action: Gina decided she might just as well have faith that if there's a relationship out there for her, she doesn't have to work to find it because it will find her!

Advice

At this point we introduced Gina to Madame Dora and asked if she'd like to pick a card to get some dating advice. Without looking, she picked Optimistic Olivia, who says, "Look for the gift in every experience. This time you'll get what you want by expecting the best that can happen. The universe is on your side and what you want is coming your way."

Talk to Your Inner Child

Gina could say to her four-year-old inner child, "Your piggy back ride is just about the corner!"

Now It's Your Turn

To learn more about yourself, fill out the template below. Follow the instructions above to guide you. You may want to invite friends or family members to help you, especially with brainstorming when you get the sections called "Private Logic" and "Advice".

Name:_____ Date:_____

Present

Current Issue: _____

_____

Past

Childhood memory: _____

_____

_____

Private Logic:

I _____

Others _____

Life_____

Therefore _____

Future

If Nothing Changes: _____

3 A's

Awareness: _____

Acceptance: _____

Action: _____

Advice

Magic Wand: _____

Madame Dora Card: _____

Thoughts:_____

Talk to Your Inner Child:_____

_____

_____

_____

_____

Conclusion
Now It's Your Turn

This book is designed to accompany *Do It Yourself Therapy*[2] and *To Know Me is to Love Me*[3] to make up the curriculum used by Encouragement Consultants. Author Lynn Lott's goal has always been to make people's lives better and to increase the ways they encourage themselves and others. She spends most of her waking hours helping people feel better and do better. She created a model called Encouragement Consultants (EC), for people who have the desire to grow and change and to be open to possibilities. If you have the desire to grow and become aware of what is happening around you and your part in all of it, and if you can accept without judgement that what is, *is*, many options present themselves. Options include actions like changing your thoughts, changing your feelings, and/or changing your behavior. Since your thoughts, feelings and behaviors are all inter-linked, if you change one, all the rest change, too.

All of this can be done without drugs, though modern day thinking would have you believe otherwise. EC is an encouragement and empowerment model, rather than a disease model. We believe that when your relationships are not working (whether with your kids, spouses, friends, family, work colleagues or yourself) it's because you're discouraged, not sick. If that's true, then you need to *look for ways to feel encouraged and to encourage others*. There are many!

One of the goals of the EC program is to help you connect with your inner child and then find ways the child is feeling discouraged. With your life skills and other skills you've learned studying works such as *The Individual Psychology of Alfred Adler* by Alfred Adler, *Children the Challenge* by Rudolf Dreikurs, and books by Jane Nelsen, Lynn Lott and others, such as the *Positive Discipline* series, you can heal your inner child, changing discouragement to encouragement and helping your inner child grow into a healthy adult.

EC is spreading around the world and is especially popular in China, Mexico, and South America. There are many opportunities to learn how

---

2 Lynn Lott & Barbara Mendenhall, 2015

3 Lynn Lott, Marilyn Matulich Kentz & Dru West, 2015

to use EC to encourage yourself and others and to become part of this growing field. For more information, you can check out Lynn's website at www.lynnlottec.com or contact her by email at lynnlott@sbcglobal.net.

www.ingramcontent.com/pod-product-compliance
Lightning Source LLC
Chambersburg PA
CBHW021940040426
42448CB00008B/1168